Too Many Rabbits

and Other Fingerplays About Animals, Nature, Weather, and the Universe

by Kay Cooper

Illustrated by Judith Moffatt

Cartwheel
·B·O·O·K·S·®

SCHOLASTIC INC.

New York Toronto London Auckland Sydney

In memory of Jim Roginski
—K.C.

For my sister, Susan, with love
—J.M.

Acknowledgments

The publisher has made diligent efforts to trace the ownership of all copyrighted material in this volume, and believes that all necessary permissions have been secured. If any errors have inadvertently been made, proper corrections will gladly be made in future editions.

"Fireflies," "Bear in a Cave," "Earth Goes Round" from *Children's Counting-Out Rhymes, Fingerplays, Jump-Rope and Bounce-Ball Chants and Other Rhymes: A Comprehensive English Language Reference* © 1983 Gloria T. Delamar by permission of McFarland & Company, Inc., Publishers, Jefferson, NC 28640.

"Little Frog," "Baby Seeds," "Trees," "Clouds," "Raindrops," "The Sun" reprinted from *Ring a Ring o' Roses*, published by the Flint Public Library, Flint, Michigan. (313) 232-7111.

"The Funny, Fat Walrus" from *Finger Frolics* © 1976 Liz Cromwell and Dixie Hibner by permission of Partner Press Inc., Livonia, Michigan 48153-0124.

"Dig A Little Hole" and "Boom! Bang! Thunder!" from *Little Boy Blue* © 1966 Western Publishing Company, Inc. Used by permission.

"Two Little Apples" from *Let's Do Fingerplays* © 1962 Marion Grayson by permission of Robert R. Luce, Inc., Manchester, New Hampshire 03102.

"Grandma Moon" from *Fingerplay Friends: Action Rhymes for Home, Church, and School* by Audrey Olson Leighton, Judson Press, Valley Forge, Pennsylvania, © 1984. Used by permission of the author.

"Johnny's Ride to Mars" from *Listen! and Help Tell the Story* by Bernice Wells Carlson, Abingdon Press, Nashville, TN 37203 © 1965. Used by permission of the author.

Cut paper illustrations photographed by Paul Dyer.

Text copyright © 1995 by Kay Cooper.
Illustrations copyright © 1995 by Judith Moffatt.
All rights reserved. Published by Scholastic Inc.
CARTWHEEL and the CARTWHEEL BOOKS LOGO
are registered trademarks of Scholastic Inc.

Library of Congress Cataloging-in-Publication Data

Cooper, Kay.
    Too many rabbits and other fingerplays : about animals, nature, weather, and the
universe / by Kay Cooper ; illustrated by Judith Moffatt.
        p.   cm.
    ISBN 0-590-45564-8
    1. Science—Experiments—Juvenile literature. 2. Finger plays—Juvenile literature.
[1. Animals. 2. Botany. 3. Weather. 4. Astronomy. 5. Finger plays.] I. Moffatt, Judith, ill.
II. Title. III. Title: Too many rabbits.
Q164.C67   1995
500—dc20   94-39720
                                                                  CIP
                                                                                     AC

12 11 10 9 8 7 6 5 4 3 2   5 6 7 8 9/9 0/0

Printed in Singapore

First Scholastic printing, September 1995

WhEn children use fingerplays to imitate falling leaves, a twinkling star, or fluttering snowflakes, they begin to understand science. This book, which contains 22 fingerplays, introduces children to scientific information and concepts about animals, nature, weather, and the universe.

The commentary following each fingerplay expands on the concept being presented and provides interesting facts and information. Through interactive play, children will delight in the fun of the fingerplays while learning about their world at the same time.

Table of Contents

Too Many Rabbits

 Gail and Sue had two little rabbits,
Two little rabbits, two little rabbits.
Gail and Sue had two little rabbits—

 Bing and

 Bong.

 Gail and Sue had four little rabbits,
Four little rabbits, four little rabbits.
Gail and Sue had four little rabbits—

 Ding and

 Dong.

 Gail and Sue had six little rabbits,
Six little rabbits, six little rabbits.
Gail and Sue had six little rabbits—

 King and

 Kong.

Gail and Sue had eight little rabbits,
Eight little rabbits, eight little rabbits.
Gail and Sue had eight little rabbits—

 Ping and

 Pong.

 Gail and Sue had ten little rabbits,
Ten little rabbits, ten little rabbits.
Gail and Sue had ten little rabbits—

 Sing and

 Song.

 All together they had
Too many rabbits,
Too many rabbits,
TOO MANY RABBITS!

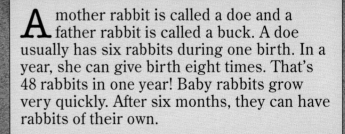

A mother rabbit is called a doe and a father rabbit is called a buck. A doe usually has six rabbits during one birth. In a year, she can give birth eight times. That's 48 rabbits in one year! Baby rabbits grow very quickly. After six months, they can have rabbits of their own.

Fireflies

 Winking, blinking, winking, blinking.
See that little light.

 Now it's here.

 Now it's there.

 Now it's out of sight.

 Winking, blinking, winking, blinking.
Fireflies at night.

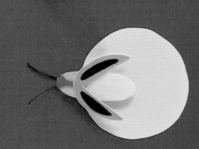

Fireflies are really not flies at all—they are beetles! The flashing light in the firefly's tail is caused by special chemicals in its body. These chemicals mix with oxygen, a gas in the air, and produce a light. That's why fireflies are also known as lightning bugs. There are about 125 kinds of fireflies in the United States and Canada.

Little Frog

A little frog in a pond am I.

Hoppity, hoppity, hop.

And I can jump in the air so high.

Hippity, hippity, hop.

Powerful hind leg muscles allow some frogs to leap many times their own body length. Their sticky hind feet grip surfaces and keep the frogs from slipping as they jump. A frog's tongue is also sticky and helps it to catch flies.

The Owl in the Barn

 A little boy went into a barn,

 And lay down on some hay.

 An owl came out and flew about,

 And the little boy ran away.

An owl usually lives alone and hunts for food at night. Owls can be a great help to farmers because they eat rats and mice that are harmful to farmers' crops. An owl's feathers, which are frayed on the edges, quiet the sound of its flapping wings. This allows the owl to silently swoop down on its prey. Owls usually build their nests in hollow trees, caves, or deserted houses and barns.

Bear in a Cave

 Here is a cave, inside is a bear.

 Now he comes out to get some fresh air.
He stays out all summer in sunshine and heat.

 He hunts in the forest for berries to eat.

When snow starts to fall

He hurries inside

His warm little cave and there he will hide.

When spring comes again,
The snow melts away

And out comes the bear ready to play.

He stays out all summer in sunshine and heat.
He hunts in the forest for berries to eat.

Bears find shelter during the cold winter months. Black bears stay in caves or in holes underneath the roots of fallen trees. Brown bears dig holes for themselves, while polar bears hollow out snowbanks.

The walrus lives in the Arctic where the weather is icy and very cold. Under its thick, wrinkled skin is a layer of fat, called *blubber*, which helps keep the walrus warm. A walrus's tusks may grow to over three feet long! The tusks are made of ivory and are often used to dig for food and to open breathing holes in the ice.

The Funny, Fat Walrus

 The funny, fat walrus sits in the sea

 Where the weather is freezing
And cold as can be.

 His whiskers are droopy

 And his tusks are white.

 And he doesn't do much but
Sit day and night.

Baby Seeds

In a milkweed cradle
Snug and warm,

Baby seeds are hiding,
Safe from harm.

Open wide the cradle.

Hold it high.

Come, Mr. Wind,
Help them fly.

Seeds are scattered in many ways. They can be carried far from the parent plant by wind, animals, water, and even people! Some seeds, such as dandelion and willow seeds, have fluffy coverings that help them to be carried by the wind. Other seeds have tiny spines or sticky coatings that can stick to the fur of an animal or to people's clothing.

Dig a Little Hole

 Dig a little hole.

 Plant a little seed.

 Pour a little water.

 Pull a little weed.

 Up! Up! Up!
Green stems climb.

 Open wide. It's blossom time!

The beginning of a new plant is curled up inside a seed. The outside seed coat protects the seed inside. A seed must be placed in or on soil for it to grow. It also needs water to soften the seed coat. When the sun shines, the seed breaks through the softened seed coat and begins to grow. Roots grow down into the soil and take in water and nutrients. The stem and leaves grow above the soil.

There are about 20,000 kinds of trees. Some may live for thousands of years and grow taller than 30-story buildings! A tree will continue to grow as long as it lives. The leaves of a tree make the food that helps the tree to grow. When fall comes, many types of trees lose their leaves and rest for the winter. Then, in the spring, they grow new leaves and flowers. Other trees, like the pine tree, have "needles" that are constantly replaced throughout the year. Because they keep their needles, these trees are sometimes called evergreens.

Trees

Elm trees stretch and stretch so wide.

Their limbs reach out on every side.

Pine trees stretch and stretch so high.

They very nearly reach the sky.

Willows droop and droop so low.

Their branches sweep the ground below.

September Leaves

 Leaves are floating softly down;
Some are red and some are brown.

 The wind goes swish through the air.

 When you look back,
There are no leaves there.

The most important job of a leaf is to make food for plants. This process is known as *photosynthesis*. Leaves are green because they contain *chlorophyll*, which reacts with sunlight and creates food for the plant. When fall arrives, the shorter days and colder temperatures cause the chlorophyll to break down, and let other colors in the leaf show through. This is why you can see red, yellow, and gold leaves during the fall months. As the chlorophyll continues to break down, the leaves stop making food, turn brown, and die.

There are many varieties of apples, each with its own unique taste. From McIntosh apples to Golden Delicious to Jonathan apples, this popular fruit fills many needs. Apples can be eaten fresh, cooked, or canned. They may also be made into juice or used to make vinegar. And, of course, they are used to make a favorite dessert — apple pie!

Two Little Apples

 Way up high in the apple tree,

 Two little apples smiled down at me.

 I shook that tree as hard as I could.

 Down came the apples.

 Ummmmmm! Good!

Wind

The wind came out to play one day.

It swept the clouds out of its way.

It blew the leaves and away they flew.

The trees bent low and their branches did, too.

The wind blew the great big ships at sea.

And it blew my kite away from me.

Wind is moving air. Although you can't see the wind, you can feel it blowing against your face. You can see what the wind does by watching objects move around you. A gentle wind carries a kite up toward the sky. A strong wind can blow an umbrella out of your hands. The strongest winds may form tornadoes, which can move houses and cars through the air!

Clouds

 What's fluffy white and floats up high,

 Like piles of ice cream in the sky?

 And when the wind blows hard and strong,

 What very gently flows along?

 What seems to have lots of fun,

 Peek-a-booing with the sun?

 When you look up in the sky,

 What do you see floating by?

Clouds are made from water that is in the air we breathe. We can't see the water because it is a gas called *water vapor*. Water vapor forms when oceans, rivers, and lakes are warmed by the sun. This vapor rises high into the sky in a process called *evaporation*. The cooler air in the sky turns the water vapor into tiny water droplets or ice crystals. When millions of these crystals or water droplets float together, a cloud is formed.

Fog

 Softly, softly creeps the fog,

 Brushing through the trees.

 It touches the grass with fingers light,

 And breathes white smoke on me.

Fog is a cloud of water droplets. It is different from the clouds in the sky because it touches the earth. Fog is formed when the air temperature cools. Water is in the air in the form of gas or vapor. Cooler air cannot hold as much water vapor as warm air, and the vapor condenses to form water droplets. The result is a ground-level cloud, or fog.

Raindrops

I listen to the raindrops fall
On thirsty trees and flowers.

I hear the rain, "pit-pat, pit-pat."

I'm so thankful for the showers.

In warm clouds, tiny water droplets bump into each other and form larger and larger drops of water. When these drops become too heavy to stay in the cloud, they fall to the ground as rain. It takes thousands and thousands of these tiny water droplets to make one raindrop.

Boom! Bang! THUNDER!

Boom, bang, boom, bang!

Rumpety, lumpety, bump!

Zoom, zam, zoom, zam!

Clippety, clappety, clump!

Lightning is a large electrical flash in the sky. When lightning flashes, it heats the air around it, which causes the air to expand in all directions. When this warm air collides with the cooler, surrounding air, it forms a giant air wave that creates the sound of a clap of thunder.

Rustles and bustles

And swishes and zings.

What wonderful noises
A thunderstorm brings!

Inside cold clouds, freezing ice crystals stick together and form snowflakes. When snowflakes become heavy, they fall to the ground as snow. Each snowflake has six points or sides. No two snowflakes ever look exactly alike.

Snowflakes

 Merry little snowflakes
Do their very best

 To make a soft, white blanket
So buds and flowers may rest.

 But when the bright spring sunshine

 Says it's come to stay,

 Those merry little snowflakes

 Quickly run away.

Earth Goes Round

 Earth is round;

 Goes round and round.
Goes round and round.

 Oh, earth is round.

The earth is a giant ball that is covered with water, rock, and dirt. Earth is always turning, or rotating. When the part of the earth that you live on turns toward the sun, it is day. When it turns away from the sun, it is night. One complete rotation of the earth is equal to one day, or 24 hours.

The Sun

 Over there the sun gets up

 And marches all the day.

 At noon it stands right overhead,

 And at night it goes away.

The sun is actually a star, made up of super-hot gases. It is the closest star to the earth, and its heat and light enable us to live on our planet. The sun rises in the east and sets in the west. Like earth, the sun rotates on its axis. It takes about one month for the sun to complete one rotation.

"Grandma Moon" is the first-quarter moon. It rises near noon and is high in the sky at sunset.

Grandma Moon

 Grandma Moon, Grandma Moon,

 You're up too soon!

 The sun is still in the sky.

 Go back to bed,

 And cover up your head,

 And wait till the day goes by.

Dog Star

 Dog Star, Dog Star, oh so high.

 You follow the hunter in the sky.

 Dog Star, Dog Star, oh so bright.

 You look blue on a clear, dark night.

A *constellation* is a group of stars that seem to form a pattern. People long ago gave these patterns names and told stories about them. Sirius, the Dog Star, is the brightest star in the night sky. It has a blue-white color and appears with several other stars to form a constellation called the Big Dog. The Big Dog follows its master, the hunter Orion. You can find Orion by looking for three bright stars in a diagonal line—they form Orion's belt.

Johnny's Ride to Mars

 Johnny looked at the moon.

 Johnny looked at the stars.

 Johnny got in a rocket.

 Johnny went to Mars.

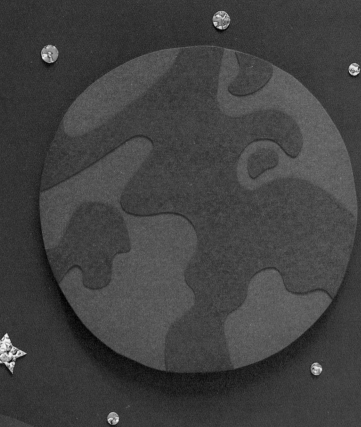

Mars appears as a small red light in the night sky. It looks red because the soil on the planet is red or rust in color. The surface of Mars has deep canyons and giant volcanoes. The largest of these volcanoes rises twice as high as earth's Mount Everest.